CW00393572

To Uncle John and Aunty Mary

From two very grateful, rested people.

Mary and Clive

AN AUSTRALIAN CAMERA
1851-1914

AN
AUSTRALIAN CAMERA
1851-1914

Michael Cannon

DAVID & CHARLES : NEWTON ABBOT
THOMAS NELSON (AUSTRALIA) LIMITED
171-5, Bank Street, South Melbourne 3205

© Michael Cannon 1973

All rights reserved. No part of this publication may be reproduced, stored in a retrieval system, or transmitted, in any form or by any means, electronic, mechanical, photocopying, recording or otherwise, without the prior permission of the publishers

This edition first published 1973
in Great Britain by
David & Charles (Holdings) Limited Newton Abbot Devon
and in Australia by
Thomas Nelson (Australia) Limited
171-5 Bank Street South Melbourne 3205
104 Bathurst Street Sydney 2000
and in Brisbane Qld, Adelaide SA and Perth WA

Thomas Nelson and Sons Ltd
36 Park Street London W1Y 4DE

Thomas Nelson and Sons (Canada) Ltd
81 Curlew Drive Don Mills Canada

ISBN 0 7153 6205 4 (Great Britain)
ISBN 17 001988 8   (Australia)

Typeset and printed in Great Britain
by W J Holman Limited Dawlish Devon

CONTENTS

LIST OF ILLUSTRATIONS

ACKNOWLEDGEMENTS

The following organisations and individuals gave a great deal of assistance in locating suitable photographs and information for use in this book:

ANZ Banking Group Ltd, Melbourne
Australian War Memorial, Canberra
Battye Library, Perth
Mr D. L. Bernstein, Melbourne
Mr John Cato, Melbourne
Commonwealth Railways, Melbourne
Country Roads Board, Melbourne
Mr B. G. Draper, Melbourne
Forestry Commission of NSW, Sydney
Mrs Dorothy Goodwin, Perth
La Trobe Library, Melbourne
Mitchell Library, Sydney
National Library, Canberra
National Trust of Australia, Melbourne
NSW Government Printer, Sydney
Oxley Memorial Library, Brisbane
Mr Cyril Pearl, Sydney
Postmaster-General's Department, Melbourne
Mr A. R. Ross, Melbourne
Royal Automobile Club of Victoria, Melbourne
Science Museum of Victoria, Melbourne
State Library of South Australia, Adelaide
Sydney University Press
Tyrrell's Bookshop, Sydney
University of Sydney Archives Department
WA Government Printer, Perth
West Australian Newspapers Ltd, Perth

INTRODUCTION

Australia, the island continent, is one of those rare countries where the major part of its occupation by white men has been recorded by the camera. Less than fifty years separated the departure of the 'First Fleet' with its British convict settlers in 1787 and Fox Talbot's invention of photography in 1834. The first daguerrotypes were made in Australia as early as 1841, and the first wet-plate negatives ten years later—just in time to record something of the great gold rushes which helped to transform the convict colonies into a vigorous modern nation. Most of the early negatives have been lost, but enough prints have survived here and there to illustrate more accurately than any other medium what happened when the British race colonised a vast isolated country occupied only by Stone Age aborigines.

As the early photographers travelled around making the portraits which were their main livelihood, they also recorded, more or less by accident, the surviving people and tumbledown buildings of the recent convict era. Perhaps even more significantly, they photographed the multitude of activities involved in establishing farms where nothing except wild bush and plain had previously existed. Together with mining, rural life in its various forms was the living core of nineteenth-century Australia. Hence it is also the core of this book.

Readers who have not visited Australia will, I hope, be able to sense some of the continent's special atmosphere through the photographs selected. The great degree of derivation from British customs and ideas is obvious at every step, but the differences are just as important. Those who have studied another book in this series, *A Country Camera 1844-1914*, dealing with rural life in Britain, will notice the similarities and differences immediately. In the English countryside, everything seems cosy and lush, but apparently frozen in its well-ordered pattern forever. In much of the Australian countryside, even today, there is a sense of vastness and isolation, of aridity and imminent peril, of desperate battling against natural forces instead of harmonious utilisation of the land.

This generally harsh environment changed the British immigrant—those who survived, that is—into an entirely different sort of person with a very different outlook on life. Where other civilisations developed courtesy and tolerance or at least obedience as social lubricants, the typical Australian remained rude, dogmatic, sardonic and xenophobic. He was as indifferent to other people's suffering as to his own hardships; and what is more, was secretly proud of all these traits. When you study the photographs towards the end of this book, showing Australians going off to take part in the wars of the old world, there is no chance of

9

mistaking them for their British forebears. The frontier has changed them for all time. I hope that this book shows something of the conditions of life which caused these fundamental changes and produced a race of men unlike any other in the world.

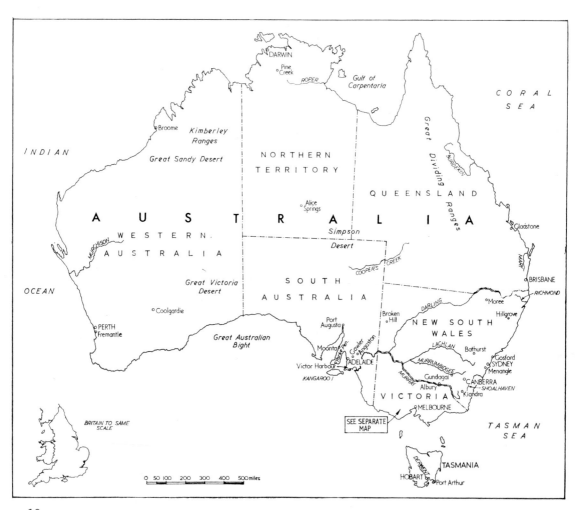

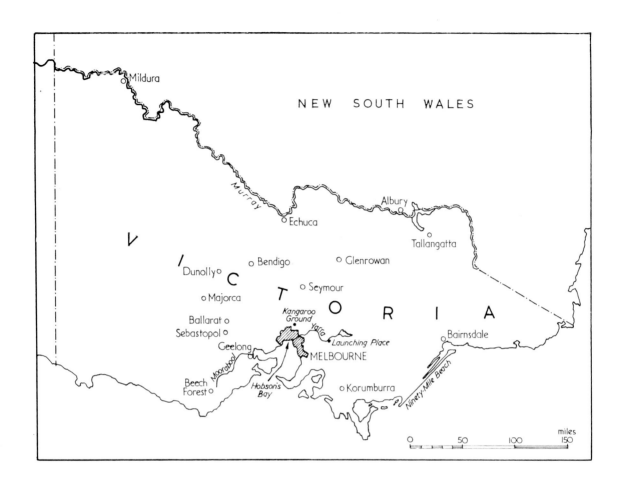

NEW SOUTH WALES

V
I
C
T
O
R
I
A

o Mildura

Murray

Albury

o Echuca

Tallangatta

o Dunolly o

o Bendigo

o Glenrowan

o Majorca

o Seymour

Ballarat o
Sebastopol o

Kangaroo
Ground

Yarra

Launching Place

o Bairnsdale

Geelong

MELBOURNE

Moorabool

Beech
Forest o

Hobson's
Bay

o Korumburra

Ninety-Mile Beach

miles
0   50   100   150

EARLY COLONIAL AND CONVICT ERA

1 This tumbledown cottage, believe it or not, was said to be Australia's first Government House. The British government founded its new convict colony on sternly economical lines. It sent Arthur Phillip, a poor boy who had risen to the rank of post captain largely by his own efforts, in charge of the 'First Fleet' with its eleven small ships and 1000 convicts and marines. Arriving in the wilderness of Sydney Cove, Phillip lived at first in a portable canvas house, but soon moved into a six-roomed cottage. The original convict-made bricks can be clearly seen here behind the crumbling stucco. Judging by the men's clothes and the horse tram rails on the roadway, this photograph would have been taken about the 1850s, when the building had been converted into a blacking factory. A foundation stone laid there commemorated Phillip's occupancy from 15 May 1788. A few months later he moved into a two-storey dwelling nearby which served a succession of British governors until 1845.

2 One of those governors, Captain William Bligh of 'Mutiny on the Bounty' fame, was forcibly deposed by rum-trading officers of the NSW Corps. After that corrupt military force was disbanded, about thirty individual British regiments served in Australia up to 1870. At first their sole task was to guard the convicts, but when fears of French or Russian invasion developed they assisted the colonists to train their own defence forces. To house the British regiments, the biggest military barracks outside the homeland was built in the centre of Sydney. Un-fortunately this began to tumble down before photography was introduced. More solid Victoria Barracks were built in stone near Sydney in 1848 and Melbourne in 1865, and are still in use today. This photograph shows officers of the 77th (East Middlesex) Foot Regiment, stationed in Sydney from 1857–8. It was taken by the first Australian-born amateur photographer, Sir William Macarthur, a prominent landowner near Sydney, and son of Captain John Macarthur who had played a leading part in deposing Governor Bligh.

3 Most of the hideous early gaols were demolished by colonists wishing to eliminate memories of their convict past. One prison which survived until the era of photography was Port Arthur, situated about sixty miles from Hobart, capital city of Tasmania. Port Arthur was known as 'the most infamous of penal stations' in the southern colony. All its buildings, ranging from tiny underground punishment cells to a magnificent Gothic church, were constructed by convicts who were then incarcerated within. One of them was Robert Pate, son of the High Sheriff of Cambridge, who had attacked Queen Victoria with his walking-stick and given her a black eye. When J. W. Beattie took this photograph of the seaward approach to Port Arthur in 1868, transportation from Britain to Tasmania had been abolished for some years. However, a few score 'lifers' and second offenders were still serving out their sentences in the rapidly deteriorating buildings.

4 Since transportation tapered off rapidly after 1840, it is almost impossible to find authenticated photographs of gaoled offenders who had been exiled from Britain to Australia. However, J. W. Beattie, as official photographer to the Tasmanian government, was permitted to photograph this convict orchestra at Port Arthur. The presence of children in the gaol was probably due to the fact that Point Puer, a nearby prison for boys, had been closed down in 1849. Also abolished was the line of hungry dogs kept chained across the entrance to the peninsula to prevent inmates escaping. Port Arthur was closed in 1877 and partially destroyed by fire some years later, although a few ruins still remain today.

1256.
WHALING. SPLITTING THE CASE.
KERRY. PHOTO. SYDNEY

5 Only three years after the first settlement of Australia by white men, several whaling ships bound for Peru took more convicts and stores to Sydney. Off the eastern coast of Australia they passed large schools of whales, and returned there to inaugurate the settlement's first important industry. Soon hundreds of tons of sperm oil were being won each year. It was said that Sydney 'stank of whaling'. Further south, the first settlements in Tasmania, Victoria and South Australia were established by roving whalers. By 1850 Hobart had become the leading whaling port in the British Empire, with thirty-seven deep-sea ships, many of them built locally by immigrants from the Hebrides. Whalers were still active in the 1880s when Charles Kerry took this photograph of whalers off New South Wales engaged in 'splitting the case'. The crew included Scots, Irish and Englishmen, as well as Chinese and Malayans who at that time were admitted fairly freely into Australian ports.

6 How many of the world's large cities can point to the first child born within their bounds? The elderly man photographed here with his wife and son was the first white child born in Melbourne, capital of Victoria. His name was John Melbourne Gilbert: both he and the city were named after Lord Melbourne who was Queen Victoria's first Prime Minister. When Gilbert was born in December 1835, son of a blacksmith, Melbourne town had about 2,000 inhabitants, mainly settlers and convicts from Tasmania. Today it has a population of nearly three million. The old slab-roofed cottages, one of which can be seen behind John Melbourne Gilbert, have given way to half a million tiled-roof private houses, practically all situated on individual quarter-acre blocks of land—a standard Australian practice which makes their cities the most sprawling in the world.

7 The first settlement after whalers in South Australia took place on Kangaroo Island, the largest island (except Tasmania) in southern Australian waters. A 'South Australian Association' was formed in 1833 to put into practice the theories of Edward Gibbon Wakefield, a London barrister who had been imprisoned for abducting a young heiress. Wakefield's idea was to sell colonial lands and use the proceeds to assist the emigration of surplus labourers. The first shiploads landed on the remote ninety-mile Kangaroo Island in 1836. Most immigrants continued on to the mainland to establish Adelaide, present-day capital of South Australia. A few, including the unidentified pioneer shown here, decided to remain. Today the island has about 2,000 inhabitants, many descended from the original English farm labourers.

8 To the north, meanwhile, the vast mysterious continent was being slowly penetrated by settlers and explorers. They included an eccentric Prussian naturalist named Ludwig Leichhardt, who had emigrated to avoid compulsory military service. Although short-sighted and unable to use a gun, Leichhardt amazed his contemporaries in 1844–5 by trekking more than 2,000 miles through unknown country from Queensland to north-western Australia. Hostile aborigines killed one of his companions and wounded two others. Leichhardt disappeared during another expedition in 1848 and no conclusive clues to his fate were ever found. Three survivors of his first expedition met some years later for this photograph. James Calvert (left) son of a Yorkshire leather manufacturer, became manager of an NSW pastoral station. Little is known of the life of John Murphy (centre), whom Leichhardt had met on shipboard, but Murphy's Range in northern Australia was named after him. John Roper (right), a native of Norfolk, England, lost an eye when the aborigines attacked. The important northern waterways of Roper River and Roper's Lakes were named after him. In later life the explorer became a stock inspector.

9 This photograph, taken about 1880, gives a good idea of the semi-arid country which lay between the lush coastal areas and the rocky inland deserts of Australia. The soil was loose and sandy, covered after occasional showers with tough native grasses and saltbush, and supporting straggling forests of eucalypts which the settlers called 'the scrub' or 'the mulga'. When overgrazed, much of this country reverted to desert. The gnarled box tree shown here at Cooper's Creek in Central Australia has a special significance. In its shade were found the bones of Robert O'Hara Burke, a brave but impulsive Irish police officer whose exploring party set off at the hottest time of the year 1860 in an attempt to cross the continent from south to north and back again. Six other men also died on the expedition, but the reports of survivors and rescue parties solved many of the mysteries of the interior, finally laying to rest tales of a fabulous ocean into which inland rivers were supposed to flow.

19

COUNTRY LIFE

10 Over vast areas of Australia the new settler's first task was to remove the forest cover so that cropping or grazing land could be created. This he achieved with the axe, the firestick, and the distinctive Australian technique of 'ring-barking'—cutting off a strip of bark all round the trunk and leaving the tree to die. Unfortunately few settlers had the foresight to leave clumps of trees to hold the soil together and provide shade for their stock. The ecological results were often disastrous. Our photograph shows a typical new farm in northern NSW, with endless paddocks of partly-burned and rotting trees. The settlers are riding in a one-horse 'jinker', a light vehicle derived from the American frontier. Its large wheels bounced easily over rough tracks and culverts, and were readily repaired. In the background can be seen the settler's cottage —a rather superior weatherboard building in this case—and uncleared bush beyond.

11 (*right*) To assist them in the arduous task of clearing and fencing the land, many settlers engaged itinerant bush workers—men who preferred to roam various parts of the country instead of settling down on their own farms. Here are two of that happy-go-lucky breed in a typical NSW bush setting. Their felt hats, full beards and remains of their ragged clothes all indicate that the picture was taken about the 1890s. Judging by their stocky build, the men were probably among the flood of labourers who emigrated from Britain: the Australian-born meat-fed 'cornstalks' were noticeably taller and leaner. The rough slab hut in the background has supports to keep it standing, and sheets of corrugated iron over the ridgecap to keep out the rain.

12 (*below*) All types from the richest to the poorest lived in these primitive bush huts during the pioneering phase. A Dr Smith—probably a surgeon who had been given a one-way passage to Australia on an immigrant ship—set up his practice in this old bush hut in 1860, and is seen here contentedly reading a book. The location was a lonely paddock on the large 'Meningoort' sheep station in western Victoria. Shepherds came from many miles around to have their ailments (usually the results of debauchery) treated with largely useless remedies. The bark roof of Dr Smith's surgery has the luxury of a calico lining, which can be seen hanging over the end wall above the timber supports. Saplings tied on with strips of greenhide stop the roof from blowing away in a gale, and the all-important ridge also consists of bark sheets. The wooden chimney at left was usually roughly lined with clay or iron to prevent it catching alight.

13 While travelling about the country, itinerant workers carried their 'swag'—a description derived from convict slang for booty, but soon applied to personal possessions. The 'swagmen' rolled their few belongings in dark blue blankets and carried them looped over one shoulder. Their roving life was known as 'humping the bluey'. The two fine-looking swagmen shown here also sported walking-sticks topped with carved rams' horns. They were photographed in the main street of Gundagai, a large sheep-town in southern NSW noted for the fact that a swagman's dog once 'shat in the tucker-box, five miles from Gundagai', thus giving rise to the words of a well-loved folk song. The short man in the centre is Charles Mudear, the local saddler. He wears elastic-sided boots which remain popular among Australian stockmen today.

14 Many swagmen were expert shearers who tramped around a regular circuit of sheep stations. They provided a pool of seasonal labour which enabled pastoralists to get vast numbers of sheep shorn before grass seeds and burrs ripened sufficiently to become embedded in the wool. Here at a South Australian woolshed is a demonstration of the technique of blade shearing which remained in vogue until the 1890s. The flat cabbage-tree hats (woven from the plant of that name), as worn by two of the grinning spectators in this photograph, indicate that it was taken not later than the 1870s, when Australia's wool production was beginning to expand enormously. With the old hand shears an expert could sometimes shear 100 sheep a day, and be paid anything from 12s 6d to £1 for the day's work. Machine shearing, invented in NSW in the late 1880s, was faster and yielded better fleeces for British woollen mills.

15 These men may look like any other un-
kempt colonial types, but in reality the
whole prestige of Australian wool exports
and hence the country's prosperity depen-
ded on their judgement. They were highly-
skilled woolclassers, working rapidly inside
the woolshed at 'Round Hill' station in
NSW in 1901. Their job was to sort the
fleeces by touch and appearance into various grades labelled AA, A, B, BB, etc for
'first combing', 'second combing', 'first clothing' and so on. Overseas buyers and wool
processors came to rely completely on the
opinions of these men working thousands
of miles away in the heat and dust of the
Australian outback.

16 The first 'squatters' in Australia were men who 'squatted' illegally on Crown lands outside the recognised limits of settlement. When their herds of stock grew to many millions their claims were legitimatised, and huge areas of the best grazing land passed with varying degrees of legality into the hands of the 'squattocracy' who became wealthy and respectable. This photograph shows 'Boodcarra', a typical residence of a successful middle-ranking squatter of the 1860s. At the extreme left are two aboriginal servants, probably the only survivors of the tribe which originally lived on the property. The next three figures are white employees who supervised the station's daily work. Next comes a crinolined governess and daughter of the household seated on her pony. The mistress, wearing an elaborate bonnet fastened with large bow, stands by her solid front door. On the right, preparing to drive off in his iron-springed buggy, is the squatter himself—John Ritchie, president of the Shire of Belfast in south-western Victoria. In the foreground, an introduced conifer struggles to establish itself in the unfamiliar environment. The house itself, with its typical shady colonial verandah, is built solidly of dressed stone. In earlier days many such homesteads had heavy shutters over the windows as protection against aboriginal attacks.

17 When the wool boom transformed squatters into wealthy men, many built lavish city mansions and appointed managers to supervise their properties. Here is the manager of 'Walla Walla' station in NSW, photographed at tea with his family on the back verandah of his cottage in 1901. This is probably the squatter's old homestead, built quite solidly with milled pine flooring and walls, with the corrugated iron roof supported by solid lengths of dried eucalypt from the bush nearby. Note the rolled-up blinds which could be lowered in bad weather to convert the verandah into additional sleeping accommodation for visitors. The large roof area and guttering collected rain water for use in the house and in the garden.

18 The only challenge to the squatters' supremacy came in the 1860s and 1870s, when radical colonial governments passed Selection Acts which were the equivalent of America's Homestead Acts. In theory the would-be farmer could 'select' half a square mile of any squatter's domain outside the block on which his house was built. Many squatters retained the waterways and fertile areas of their properties by secretly buying them up through 'dummies'. Here we see a genuine selector setting off to take up his block of land. With a horse and bullock harnessed together he would not get far; unfortunately his subsequent experiences are not on record.

19 Possibly ten per cent of selectors managed to get themselves established on the land. This Queensland settler seems to be doing well for himself. He has a neat cottage with watertight roof of split hardwood shingles and separate slab chimney. The hut even seems to have a proper floor instead of the usual mud underfoot. His wife's head is bowed under her shady straw bonnet, but she has given birth to four living children in that little hut, probably with assistance only from her husband. On average mortality rates, another three or four of her babies would have died. This photograph is by Richard Daintree, a Huntingdonshire geologist who did his best pictorial work in the Burdekin River district of Queensland in the late 1860s.

20 In some coastal areas, selectors enjoyed
high rainfall but first had to cope with
forests of gigantic eucalyptus trees. This
monster had a circumference of more than
sixty feet and was one of many between 200
and 300 feet high. Successive fires burnt out
its heart, so that a trap could be driven right
inside. The scene is the Beech Forest of
southern Victoria about 1895. The men are
typical successful dairy farmers of the area,
which not surprisingly produced some of
the world's wood-chopping champions.

21 Children in dairy-farming areas had a rugged upbringing, usually being kicked out of bed before dawn, the girls to make butter and the boys to milk the cows by hand. Sometimes they also transported the milk cans by packhorse to the nearest butter factory. Only the introduction of compulsory education in the 1870s saved them from complete slavery. Here a farm-lad walks his horse to town in the Shoalhaven River district of NSW in 1898. After attending school he will ride home again in time for the evening milking. In the depressed 1890s, the few shillings earned were sometimes all that stood between his family and destitution.

22 On the warmer black-soil plains of northern Victoria and South Australia, selectors concentrated on establishing wheat farms which came to rival the area and production of the Canadian prairies. Many technological advances were made by inventive amateurs, including the world's first successful mechanical grain strippers, 'stump-jump' ploughs, combined stripper–thresher–winnowers, and disease-resistant varieties of wheat. Here is the summer harvesting scene on Gregory's Farm, Modbury, South Australia, in 1906. Women and children, who before had to help harvest and winnow the crop by hand, now merely have the pleasant task of taking tea to the men.

THE FAR OUTBACK

23   Settlement of the arid and tropical regions of Australia was the most difficult undertaking of all, and has not been finally accomplished even today. One of the first systematic attempts was made by George Woodroofe Goyder, a London engineer who became surveyor-general of South Australia. In 1868 Goyder took a large expedition to the Northern Territory, selected Palmerston (Darwin) as the site for a capital, and surveyed more than 650,000 acres for growing tropical products. Here are some of his survey party in the tangled forest, all armed with revolvers to protect themselves against marauding aborigines. Not many 'tropical products' were ever grown in the area, but much of it became good cattle country. The picture was taken by Captain Samuel Sweet, a retired mariner who styled himself 'Professor of Photography'.

24 Port Darwin was discovered on a voyage of HMS *Beagle* in 1839 and named after Charles Darwin who had visited Australia on the ship three years earlier. After Goyder's survey, a number of primitive buildings were erected by settlers, each of whom were given one township allotment for each 320 acres of agricultural land purchased. For relaxation they thronged this bark and timber 'Commercial Hotel' in Mitchell Street. The figure nearest the camera is R. C. Patterson, one of the officers in charge of constructing an overland telegraph line which joined the British submarine cable at Darwin in 1872. A few years later a cyclone flattened the whole township. It never prospered until the Federal government took over the Northern Territory in 1911.

25 Although agriculture failed, gold strikes lured men back to the north. Gold was discovered at Pine Creek, 120 miles south-east of Darwin, in 1871. Twenty years later the town still had a solid population of nearly 1,000. To control the miners, cattlemen and native tribes nearby, strong police forces had to be maintained. Here is some of the staff at Pine Creek police headquarters in its heyday. At the rear and left front, five native troopers and two houseboys. Seated on chairs, three white troopers and one man's wife. In front, three native housegirls. The exploits of both white and black troopers in the north were often heroic but sometimes discreditable, wild aborigines occasionally being shot on mere suspicion without trial.

26 An unexpected source of wealth was discovered around the northern coastline in the form of silver- and gold-lip pearl shell, the world's most beautiful variety. Until recent times it was in great demand for the best pearl buttons and dials for ships' compasses. Broome, a port on the north-west coast of Western Australia, named after a Canadian-born squatter who became Governor of the State, was the centre of the pearling industry from the 1890s. At its peak the town had more than 5,000 residents, and 300 pearling luggers employing Japanese and Malayan divers. The two boats seen here have not been wrecked—the 28ft tidal rise and fall at Broome has merely left them stranded for a few hours. In the background, a horse dray removes pearl shell from a lugger.

27 The main wealth of the outback lay in beef cattle, which thrived on sparse vegetation and could walk long distances to water. When ready for market they were often 'overlanded'—that is, walked across the entire face of Australia to the centres of population in the south. Here we see four native stockmen rounding up cattle for the long drive. Aboriginal youths were found particularly suitable for this roving kind of life. For many years they were given nothing beyond a horse, clothes and 'tucker' (rations). Only in the last few years have serious attempts been made to force owners to pay them the same wages as white stockmen.

EXPLORING PARTY LEAVING
FOR KIMBERLY VIA WILUNA
TO OPEN UP STOCK ROUTE.
DAY DAWN. MAY 7 1906.

28 Exploration to discover better stock routes continued into the present century. In 1906 Alfred Canning, a surveyor for the WA Lands Department, led an expedition to find an overland route by which cattle could be brought from the Kimberley Ranges in the north to markets in the south. Here we see Canning nearest the camera, ready to set off with half a dozen companions, twenty camels, water supplies and stores. Within a year he had discovered a 750 mile desert route spotted with enough waterholes, soaks and bore water to keep mobs of cattle alive on the trip. The first drovers bringing down cattle in 1909 were speared to death by aborigines, and armed guards were posted to accompany further parties.

GIL GIL BORE—MOREE DISTRICT
Depth 3093 Ft.
Flow 700,000 Gals.
Temp. 112 % Fah.

29   In the eastern States, the existence of water-bearing artesian strata at depths of 1,000 feet or more was discovered in the 1880s. When holes were drilled into the rock, the water escaped at high pressure, sometimes yielding millions of gallons a day. With this discovery, stockmen were able to extend their activities further into semi-arid regions. Here is a typical bore and irrigation channel at Moree, a NSW town named after the aboriginal word meaning 'long spring'. When photographed in 1895, the bore was yielding 700,000 gallons of water a day. Finally the flow became too highly mineralised for stock. Today sufferers from rheumatism and other complaints will travel long distances to be able to bathe in the healing waters of Moree.

30   While the fashion for ostrich feather fans, boas and head-dresses lasted, some Australian settlers made extra money by breeding the birds. The first ostriches were imported from South Africa in 1865 and grazed in Victoria and NSW. Their feathers sold for about £50 per bird on the London market. The semi-arid regions of South Australia were found even more suitable for the birds, which thrived on a diet of saltbush. The SA government made a gift of 5,000 acres of this otherwise useless land to anyone who undertook to place 250 birds on it. Here is one of the ostrich farms which sprang up as a result, in desolate country a few miles north of Port Augusta. The outbreak of World War I extinguished the industry. The birds were allowed to escape: their descendants still roam the desert fringes today.

THE MINERS

31 The discovery of large gold deposits in 1851 gave an enormous stimulus to immigration and saved Australia from being completely dependent on rural products. The biggest single nugget ever discovered was the 'Welcome Stranger', found in 1869 only a few inches below the surface near Bulldog Gully, a few miles north-west of Dunolly in central Victoria. By a marvellous coincidence a photographer named Parker was nearby. He hurried to the spot and took this photograph of the discoverers with their newfound wealth. They were two Cornish miners, John Deason (holding the crowbar) and Richard Oates (holding the pick). Mrs Deason is kneeling behind the nugget. The men gave a few scraps of the nugget to their friends, then broke it into three parts to transport to the Dunolly bank, which paid them £9,500. When it was smelted, 2,268 ounces of pure gold were obtained from the find.

32 Most diggers had to be content with small particles of gold dug out of mines or panned out of river beds in auriferous country. Here we see both activities going on under the blazing sunshine. The man in the background is painfully picking a tunnel into a likely hillside, hoping to discover a payable lode. The man on the right is using a wooden tub and Californian cradle to wash the rock dug out as well as material from the creek. Gold, being heavier, sank to the bottom of the cradle and was retained. The youth at left is panning creek bed material: by swirling the dish around small nuggets were sometimes separated from the dross. The photograph was taken by Nicholas Caire, who emigrated from Guernsey to Australia in 1860.

33 When shafts had to be sunk straight down into the strata, a horse-whim arrangement like this was often used to reduce the manual labour involved. A horse was harnessed to the circular whim and driven around it all day, raising and lowering buckets of mud and ore. This device was particularly necessary where underground streams or seepage threatened to fill up the shaft. In one such Victorian shaft known as Blacksmith's Hole, a party of miners won £24,000 worth of gold after a few weeks' work.

34 The golden age was particularly beneficial to the long-depressed economy of Western Australia. Among the first discoveries were the Murchison River goldfields north of Perth, which to date have produced more than five million ounces of gold. At Mount Magnet, one of the bigger fields nearby, four successful diggers are shown celebrating Christmas Day in the 1890s. From their bough, canvas and bullock-hide hut nicknamed 'Monte Carlo' they have produced a rough table, a bowl of dried wildflowers, a loaf of home-made bread, bottles and even one wine glass. The bicycles on which they rode up the dusty 500-mile track from Perth can be seen on either side. I like to think that one man wore the boater seen hanging beside the boomerang as he pedalled through the wilderness. And did they really need that straw broom to sweep out the hut's dirt floor?

35 In 1892 Australia's greatest goldfield was discovered at Coolgardie, 350 miles east of Perth on the southern fringe of the Great Victoria Desert. Gold-hungry men disregarded the scarcity of water in the scorching area and many perished en route. Camel teams brought supplies which sold for up to 2s 6d a gallon. Within two years this extraordinary corrugated iron township had sprung up, with its own newspaper, telegraph office and stock exchange. A light railway was hastily built to transport 20,000 gallons of water a day and other necessities, and the population grew to a peak of 10,000. The field has now produced more than 35 million ounces of gold.

36 Many other minerals besides gold featured in Australian colonial development. Here is a manganese mine near the beach at Gladstone, Queensland, in 1891. The shaft with its hand-operated windlass and buckets was typical of thousands of small mining endeavours all over the country; though it was unusual so close to an established town.

37 Large deposits of copper ore were found by shepherds on 'Walleroo' and 'Moonta' stations on the Yorke Peninsula of South Australia in the early 1860s. Within a few years they had paid millions of pounds in dividends. These boys were photographed sorting ore from the mines in 1913. The squatter on whose property the deposits were found was Walter Watson Hughes, a Fifeshire-born whaler and opium trader who settled in SA in 1842. After his shepherds' discoveries had made him wealthy, Hughes donated £20,000 to found Adelaide University, was knighted as a result, and retired to Fancourt estate at Chertsey, Surrey.

IMMIGRANTS

38 During the nineteenth century immigrants of all types were allowed into Australia quite freely, although a head-tax was imposed on Chinese gold-seekers. After Federation of the States the 'White Australia Policy' was rigorously enforced, and only British immigrants were subsidised. Here is a stolid-looking group of English farm workers ready to embark for NSW in 1910. An Australian newspaper, the *Argus*, thought that 'To an Englishman or a Scot, accustomed from birth to seeing highly developed farms all about him . . . it must be somewhat disconcerting to be suddenly placed in the middle of an enormous area of virgin plain'. However, added the newspaper reassuringly, conditions had improved greatly since pioneering days, and any farmer who failed in Australia 'would not be likely to succeed anywhere else'.

39 During the days of sail there was considerable mortality on the long voyage out through disease and shipwreck. Here is the iron barque *County Antrim,* which got as far as the Ninety-Mile Beach, a long sweep of sand in Gippsland, Victoria, before it began to leak seriously during a terrific storm in 1897. The master ran his vessel into the shallows, and in this case all aboard managed to scramble safely to shore. In many other wrecks, however, early immigrants caught only a glimpse of their adopted land before being drowned.

40 So many hundreds of ships were wrecked off the Australian coast that a system of lighthouses and rescue services had to be set up at the worst danger points. Here a team of immigrants at Victor Harbour, South Australia, practises rescuing a man with rocket and breeches buoy equipment in 1894.

41 This was the view of Sydney seen by immigrants landing at Circular Quay in the 1880s. At the right is the famous clipper *Cutty Sark,* an iron-framed vessel launched on the Clyde in 1869, which once sailed from Britain to eastern Australia in sixty-four days. In 1938 the ship was presented to the Thames Nautical Training College. In the background are the stone warehouses and dwellings of early Sydney, many of them built by convict labour. Most have been demolished since this photograph was taken: the scene is almost unrecognisable today.

42 In Melbourne the immigrants were landed at Hobson's Bay railway pier. This was the same spot where tens of thousands of gold-seekers had been rowed ashore and tipped off at the beach with their belongings. Conditions had greatly improved by the 1860s, when this photograph was taken. A dozen big clippers could now tie up at the pier to unload immigrants and load up with wool for the homeward run. The steamer *Edina* at left, formerly a troopship in the Crimea, was used in Melbourne from 1863 as a passenger ferry and coastal trader. In the centre, the two-mile railway to Melbourne was the first steam service in Australia, opened in 1854. At the inaugural ceremony the locally-built engine refused to budge, and had to be pushed off the pier by twenty policemen. It was replaced by Stephenson locomotives.

43 When they went 'up country', immigrants sometimes had the choice of staying at boarding houses instead of low-grade bush pubs while they looked for work. Here in the 1880s is Mrs White's weatherboard establishment, where the sign-writer was allowed a free hand before the corrugated iron verandah was added over part of his lettering. The location was the eastern Victorian town of Bairnsdale. This was first settled by Captain Norman Macleod, who originally called it 'Bernisdale' after his native village on the Isle of Skye. In a moment of Gaelic humour he changed the name to 'Bairns-dale' because of the large number of children born there when immigrants and selectors moved in.

44 In Western Australia, immigrants landed near the spot where Captain Charles Fremantle, RN, had claimed the entire western coast of the continent in 1829 to forestall French ships cruising in the vicinity. Here is a group of British newcomers with their belongings at Fremantle Immigration Office about eighty years after the first settlement. They would find that native-born Australians would at first scorn their old-country ways, calling them 'poms' or 'pommies'. The epithet was possibly derived from the initials POME ('Prisoner of Mother England') written in early immigration records beside the names of convicted men. A more flattering theory is that their rosy cheeks were like pomegranates, a word used in an early verse to rhyme with 'jimmygrants' (immigrants).

45 German immigrants played a surprisingly large part in the settlement of Australia. Here are some of the thousands of German gold-seekers who went to the diggings. They are seen outside their club house in Majorca, a Victorian gold-rush town which has since disappeared from the map. In this early photograph the hairdresser with his two striped poles is still in business, but the larger shingle-roofed building next door already seems to be falling into disrepair. Most of the 40,000 Germans who settled in Australia by the end of the century took up farming and wine-growing. Many of those who were not interned on the outbreak of World War I anglicised their names.

46 Italian immigrants also formed an important segment of colonial population, particularly in viticulture, fruit-growing and sugar cane-cutting. The photograph of this Italian family at a NSW vineyard was proudly labelled 'Five Generations of Italian Stock'. One area of the Richmond River district of northern NSW became known as 'New Italy' in the 1880s. It was founded by Venetian immigrants who had been induced by C. du Breil, Marquis de Rays, to pioneer an island in the Bismarck Archipelago off New Guinea. Many died and the remainder fled in desperation to NSW, where they were given farming land to establish a permanent settlement.

TRANSPORT

47 The stock horse was a mainstay of Australian life, bred in great numbers on the rolling paddocks and bushlands until by 1900 there was about one mount for every adult male in the continent. Here are three splendid examples of stock horses and their riders outside the little settlement of Kangaroo Ground (Vic) in the 1860s. These animals were completely tireless, being accustomed to rounding up cattle at the gallop or carrying a heavy rider up to 100 miles a day. Hand-feeding was almost unknown: they lived off the tough native grasses and whatever water they could find. Many thousands of such horses were sold to the British Army in India for use as cavalry remounts.

48 Many wide rivers along the eastern sea-board could only be crossed by punt until quite recent years. Here is a peaceful scene on the Mary River in Queensland showing one of the first privately-operated punts in the 1870s. In the background, a settler has partly cleared the scrub, left the stumps standing, and built his cottage. At the right, a bush road leads down to the water's edge where two children in white smocks play. In the foreground, two men stand on a punt built of saplings and rough planks, and are driven across by a tiny steam boat. Many settlers operated such punts to add to their cash income, charging a small toll to ferry passengers and stock across. By the end of the century nearly all punts had been taken over by government authorities.

49 In extremely muddy areas like south-eastern Victoria, settlers used horse drawn sleds to transport passengers, milk cans and so on. The 'Korumburra Sledge' shown here had a regular route through the district during winter, enabling this mother to take her babe-in-arms to visit neighbours. Once known as 'the wild cattle run', the area had an annual rainfall of about 50 inches. It was heavily timbered with 200-foot bluegum and black-butt trees until selectors burned vast areas to establish their farms.

50 In its south-eastern pastoral section, Australia was fortunate in possessing a vast system of waterways consisting of the Darling, Murrumbidgee and Murray rivers. Paddleboats began plying on them in 1853, and within a few years scores of large and small steamers were operating regular services along four thousand miles of river—more than double the navigable length of the Mississippi. Here is a typical locally-built steamer, the *Emily Jane*, carrying passengers, bags of wheat and live sheep in the 1890s. During the shearing season the boats towed huge barges stacked high with wool bales bound for Britain.

51 River-boat traffic was almost extinguished by competition from railways by the end of the century. More than 10,000 miles of lines of various gauges had been built throughout Australia by 1890, much of the work being financed by British capital and built by British engineers. Great bridges and tunnels had to be constructed through difficult country. Here a new viaduct over the Moorabool River at Geelong (Vic) is tested in 1894 by running locomotives on to it from both ends. Officials show their faith in the quality of the job by posing underneath for the camera.

52   In the cities, horses remained the most common means of transport until well into the new century. Here we see a great variety of horse-drawn vehicles in George Street, the main commercial artery of Sydney, looking south about 1895. At left, two 'sulkies' (jinkers with hoods) and a hansom cab can be seen. In the centre are several horse buses, with slatted seats on top enabling passengers to sit and enjoy the sunshine. At right are delivery drays, and a wagon laden with bales of wool heading for Circular Quay. At right is the famous bookshop of Geo Robertson & Co, biggest Australian outlet for English books for many years. Not only reading matter but also city architecture was almost completely derived from English sources.

53 In motoring, Australians took an early lead. Herbert Thomson, a young Melbourne engineer, designed this 5hp kerosene-heated steam car in 1896. He is seen here two years later taking his family for a drive. In 1900 Thomson took the car on the first overland motor trip from Bathurst (NSW), travelling the 500 miles over rough bush roads at an average speed of nine miles an hour and a cost of a penny per mile. Thomson named his car 'the Royal', got its maximum speed up to 25mph, and sold models to fire brigades, post offices and shire councils.

54 Since Australians had vast distances to cover, aviation fascinated them from very early days. The first successful Australian-built aeroplane was this model seen flying at Bendigo (Vic) racecourse in 1911. It was designed, built and flown by John Duigan, a squatter's son who had studied engineering at Finsbury Technical College in London. Duigan got hold of a picture of the Wright Brothers' machine in 1907 and began copying it in a lean-to shed on his father's property, using ordinary farm tools.

He imported a 20hp air-cooled engine, improved it by adding water-cooled heads, and designed his own propellor. Then he made a light frame of pliable mountain ash, and designed the first air springs used for landing gear. His first flight of 200 yards took place in a cleared paddock on 7 October 1910: a local newspaper described the plane's 'mad rush through the air' at 25mph. Duigan served with the Australian Flying Corps in France during World War I and won the Military Cross.

COMMUNICATIONS

55 Postal communications in more remote areas of the continent were dependent for nearly a hundred years on horse-drawn coaches. These gave a touch of the American West to the comparatively peaceful Australian countryside. Indeed they were introduced by an American named Freeman Cobb, who took two prototypes with him during the gold rush and had hundreds of similar coaches built in Australia. By the end of the century Cobb & Co operated the world's biggest system—7,000 miles of regular routes—30,000 horses to pull the coaches. Here is the mail coach outside the post office, store and bush inn at Launching Place, a small farming settlement outside Melbourne. Stout leather springs enabled them to cross the roughest roads.

MEETING
THE MAILMAN.
397. Kerry. Sydney.

56 From wayside mail drops the precious pouches of letters and newspapers were carried by teams of horsemen out to the remotest farms and sheep stations—even to drovers taking mobs of stock on lonely 1,000 mile treks. The mailman was a universally welcome visitor at any homestead or campfire, for the mail he brought was often the only way in which isolated settlers could keep in touch with the outside world. Here a smartly turned out mailman with leggings, jodphurs and Stetson hat makes a delivery beside a billabong (lagoon) in NSW. The squatter's wife is wearing a shady spoonbill straw hat with her simple blouse and skirt, dating the photograph as early 1900s.

57 City deliveries of parcels were often left in the hands of private contractors, who competed fiercely to get goods off newly-arrived ships and through the colonial customs departments. The Western Australian service seen here picked up small consignments from English ships when they first touched the continent at Fremantle, and galloped the twelve miles to Perth with the latest dress samples, London journals, and so on. Behind them is a carriage-building works of the type found in practically every colonial township.

58 Telegraphic communication was maintained with England and over a vast internal network by small groups of 'lightning squirters' (Morse code operators) manning lonely relay stations. By 1891 Victorians alone were sending three million telegrams a year. Here is an isolated log-and-daub station, built near Darwin in 1871 to re-transmit messages to and from London. These outposts were often attacked by aborigines: the long rifle held by the pipe-smoking guard was no mere ornament.

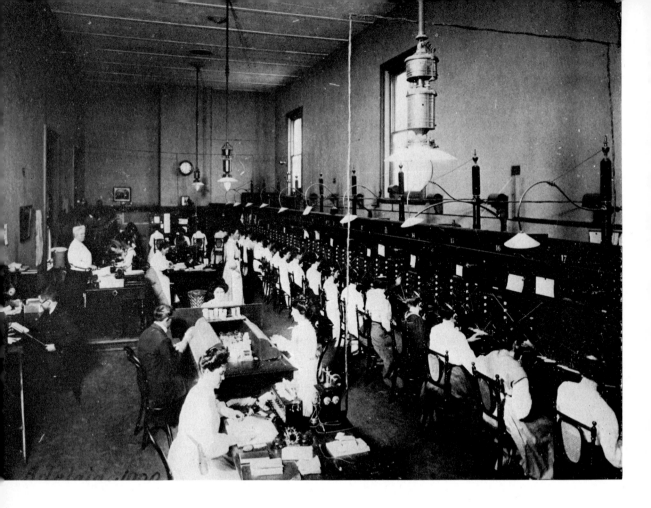

59 Australians also leaped on to the invention of the telephone to help overcome the distance problem. Experimental models were operating in Melbourne in 1877, only a year after Alexander Graham Bell announced his invention. The first long-distance phone calls were demonstrated in South Australia (240 miles) and NSW (140 miles) in 1878. By 1880 exchanges with hundreds of subscribers had been opened in the larger capital cities and towns. Here is the Adelaide exchange in 1909, which not only handled calls from all over the continent but also gave welcome employment to many of the 'New Women' who were trying to emancipate themselves.

COLOURED POPULATION

60 When the British first settled in Australia they found something like 300,000 black-skinned aborigines living a nomadic Stone Age existence. By the end of the nineteenth century there were only 40,000 left —representing genocide on an impressive scale for those days. Yet only a few thousand were killed by the settlers' guns and poisoned baits. Detribalisation, drunkenness and white men's diseases were the main causes of the disaster. Here is a typical tribe of Victorian aborigines about 1860, apparently living in a state of nature as the settlers found them. But their numbers have already been greatly diminished, and two of the boys shown here are obvious half-castes, the result of cohabitation with white shepherds or squatters.

61 Many peaceful aborigines were dressed up in white man's clothes, given regular rations, and used as cheap labour to supplement white immigrants, who often preferred to stay in the cities. Here a group of aborigines from Point McLeay Mission Station in South Australia earn their keep by drying scoured wool for a local squatter. Sometimes the urge to 'go walkabout' seized them, and they would simply melt away into the bush, reappearing casually for more 'tucker' after a few weeks.

62 Christmas 'treats' for the vanishing race consisted of the gift of one blanket each per year in the name of Queen Victoria, or the issue of extra rations. At Alice Springs telegraph station in the centre of the continent, ingredients for 'Christmas pudding' were mixed in a large galvanised iron container and taken away in liquid form by these native women and children. They came to depend on such handouts and lost their native arts of survival in the wilderness.

63 Among the saddest results of the era were full-blood and half-caste waifs, abandoned by their own drunken and diseased parents, and cared for only by the sporadic efforts of voluntary charity workers. Here are some of the results, taken off the streets of Sydney and lined up in an unknown photographer's studio for this pathetic study. The little man with thumbs hooked firmly in his wrinkled waistcoat seems determined to make his way in the harsh world, but the blurred figure on the right holds his friend's hand for reassurance in these strange surroundings.

64 When aborigines failed them, settlers often employed Chinese for labouring duties on farm and station. Here are two Chinese helping to scour wool at a steam-washing plant on a NSW sheep station. They were also widely used as station cooks. The Chinese originally emigrated to search for gold. By 1888 there were 50,000 in Australia, many of them used by employers as 'free labour' to break shipping and shearing strikes by white workers' unions.

65 Although the Chinese only brought a few women with them, busy 'Chinatowns' grew up in Sydney and Melbourne by the end of the century. Their inhabitants lived by importing Chinese products, manufacturing furniture, tending market gardens, opening Chinese restaurants, and occasionally supplying opium to addicts. Here are some locally-born Chinese–Australians in Melbourne at the turn of the century, when all further immigration of coloured races was prohibited.

66 In Queensland, meanwhile, sugar plant-
ers were encouraging the activities of 'black-
birders', who brought them cheap 'kanaka'
labour from the Pacific islands. Masters of
Royal Navy vessels denounced the trade as
'kidnapping' and 'murder', but it continued for many years with the connivance
of Queensland governments controlled by
plantation owners and squatters. John
Lindt, a Melbourne photographer, accom-
panied one 'recruiting' trip to the New
Hebrides in the 1880s. He took this remark-
able picture of an armed native bringing
a bound captive for sale to members of
the ship's crew. Once in Queensland the
'recruit' might be paid a few shillings a
month and returned home after three years
—or he might join the 10,000 formerly
healthy Polynesians who died on the plan-
tations there.

67 Unknown numbers of island women
were also 'recruited' for purposes of prosti-
tution or to work in the canefields as shown
here. The Rev William Gray reported in
1895 that pregnant women were forced to
continue working in the cane up to the day
their babies were born. Even going by the
Queensland government's own figures, the
mortality rate among these coloured workers was ten times that of the white population in the same age groups. One of the first
actions of the new Federal Government in
1901 was to ban all kanaka immigration
and return the surviving islanders to their
homes.

TOWN LIFE

68   The development of country towns brought the first taste of community life into the Australian wilderness. This fascinatingly detailed photograph by J. W. Lindt shows an unnamed mountain township in process of transformation from scattered slab huts to something approaching civilisation. The large building with verandah is the hotel, usually the town's focal point. Two horses are tied up outside while their owners buy liquor in the American-type bar-room. One child stands on the verandah: a woman holding another child waits on the muddy track outside. In the background are dozens of tiny huts, mostly with mud floors, in which the residents lived a comfortless existence. In the foreground, a tree across the stream serves as a primitive bridge. At left, the town's first 'post and rail' fence is similar to those which enclosed many thousands of square miles of grazing land.

69 This photograph shows even more clearly how towns grew up around the first inns. This is Sebastopol, a small settlement south of Ballarat, Victoria. The town was named after the famous siege of the Crimean War; its muddy thoroughfare was called Albert Street after Queen Victoria's consort. Mick Sullivan's weatherboard National Hotel in the centre was probably the town's first inn. Alongside, William Bray has built his Victoria Hotel in brick, no doubt supplied from the kiln whose chimney can be seen at left. At right, a clothing store with samples hanging out in the weather completes a typical Australian town scene of about 1860.

70 At its peak in the 1860s, the central Victorian town of Majorca boasted a population of 15,000 and a thrice-daily Cobb coach service to nearby provincial cities. Today it has completely disappeared from the map. The London Chartered Bank at left, which bought large quantities of gold for shipment to England, collapsed in the depression of the 1890s, hundreds of similar branches also closing down. In this scene, the leather-aproned butcher next door displays sides of meat for sale in the dust and hot sun—the usual unhygienic custom of the times. The next building is a cheap eating-house, whose waistcoated proprietor looks prosperous enough.

71 As gold production declined, more permanent towns grew up based on pastoral and agricultural wealth. Here a load of wool from Ellesmere station in eastern Victoria is taken by horse wagon through a country town which has attained its final form. The road has been firmly metalled and kerbs constructed. The old two-storey hotel with its intricate cast-iron lace has been converted into a respectable restaurant. In the background, a National Bank built in stone shows its faith that this is not just another ghost town. If you substitute modern dress and motor vehicles, you are not far from the appearance of many Australian towns today.

72 The well-watered plains of central NSW supported many prosperous townships. Here is J. Jaye & Co's galvanising and tinplating establishment in Bathurst about 1872. British migrants who brought skills like this were greatly valued. Mr Jaye combined his advertising signs with the admonition to 'Live and Let Live', but whether this was a plea for remission of sins or for additional trade is not known. This photograph gives a good idea of the rough street conditions even in larger towns of the period: the pillar-box seems likely to topple into the mud at any moment.

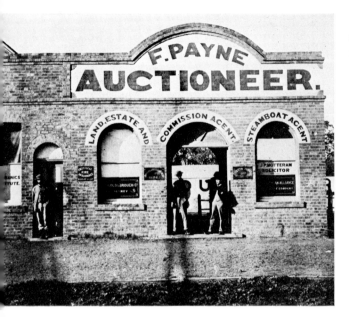

73 A few inland river towns grew to respectable size. At the junction of three major rivers, the town of Echuca (aboriginal for 'meeting of the waters') was at one time the second busiest port in Victoria, although situated 150 miles from the nearest ocean. In this riverside building, many aspects of colonial town life can be seen. At left is the entrance to the local Mechanics' Institute, an important factor in the age of self-improvement. Next door, F. Payne seems to carry on every conceivable type of real estate, customs, steamboat and insurance agency work. Conveniently, a solicitor occupies one corner, for even in those frontier days legal disputation was a popular pastime.

74 Here is a typical Australian country town of the 1890s, with well-established private buildings but primitive public facilities such as roads and sanitation. In this case the town is Gosford, a dairying and timber-cutting centre fifty miles north of Sydney. It was named by a NSW Governor, Sir George Gipps, after his friend the second Earl of Gosford. In these rather uninspiring surroundings the well-known nineteenth-century Australian poet Henry Kendall wrote much of his best work. A 100 acre historical museum recreating convict Sydney is now being built near Gosford.

75   Here is the prosperous wool city and port of Geelong, western Victoria, in the 1850s, with the settlers' covered wagons bringing their first produce to the town's new market square. John Batman, son of a transported convict, purchased 100,000 acres of this land from the aborigines, paying them with a few blankets and mirrors. The government disallowed the transaction and took the land for nothing, ultimately reselling it to squatters at high prices. One of the first permanent settlers in this area was that rare phenomenon, the lady squatter—Anne Drysdale, sister of the Treasurer of Edinburgh. The Austin family from Glastonbury, Somerset, also owned large properties nearby. On returning to England in 1854, James Austin presented Geelong with this charming clock tower, which stood until 1923. But he also sent out two dozen wild grey rabbits to his brother. These rapidly bred into several hundred millions, which over-ran the entire continent's best grazing land.

CITY LIFE

76 Where they possessed permanent gold mines or had strong pastoral backing, a few Australian inland towns were able to grow into important provincial cities. Here is a street scene of the 1860s in Ballarat, site of some of the richest gold discoveries in Victoria. By 1870 the city had a population of 60,000, with 300 companies exploiting deep lodes of gold-bearing quartz. The native word 'Ballaarat' was said to mean 'resting on the elbow': possibly it was from this phrase that the expression 'bending the elbow' (having a drink) was derived. Appropriately, the Georgian building on the right is the original Craig's Royal Hotel, with its more lavish boom-time additions in the centre. In 1867 this was described as the colony's finest hotel, being the favourite meeting-place for wealthy mine-owners. Some of these early immigrants who 'struck it rich' can be seen at their ease on the first floor balcony.

SYDNEY, FROM NORTH SHORE

77 Only the seaports could grow beyond the gold cities' size into State capitals. This photograph shows how Sydney (named after Lord Thomas Sydney, Colonial Secretary at the time of the 'First Fleet') had grown by 1900 into a major city strung around its long harbour shoreline. The view is taken from the area known as the 'North Shore' opposite Governor Phillip's original place of settlement. In the foreground, school-boys push a toy boat around one of many pools in the sandstone on which Sydney is built. Regular ferry services from the North Shore to the city began in 1849, and the population expanded rapidly. Not until nearly 100 years later (1932) was the huge Sydney Harbour Bridge opened to connect north and south shores.

78 (*above*) Although Australia's second city, Hobart did not go through the same rapid transformation as most mainland cities. Founded in 1804 as a penal settlement on the remote southern island of Van Diemen's Land (Tasmania), Hobart spread out slowly from its scattered convict buildings, whaling depots, warehouses and mills. It was named after Lord Robert Hobart, Colonial Secretary in 1804. J. W. Beattie probably took this photograph of Hobart in the 1860s. Although the city is more developed today, many of its old stone buildings remain, lending it a delightful colonial atmosphere not entirely different from this scene of a hundred years ago.

79 (*left*) By contrast, this is Collins Street in Melbourne (capital city of Victoria) which has changed beyond all recognition. The Italianate and neo-Gothic buildings of the 1880s boom have practically all given way to steel and glass skyscrapers. The delightful cable trams, once part of the world's longest system, no longer glide with 'swan-like motion' through the uncrowded streets. The roadways, once made of millions of tough jarrah wood blocks covered with a thin layer of bitumen, are now part of a concrete jungle almost indistinguishable from any other large city.

80 (*above*) Adelaide, the sunny, relaxed capital of South Australia, has had fewer economic booms than the bigger mainland capitals and is more conscious of a colonial heritage. As in Hobart, many of its original stone buildings remain. Except for the horse transportation, this picture of Rundle Street in the 1890s could almost be a main street scene today. Hundreds of acres of parklands separating the city area from its suburbs preserve Adelaide's reputation as one of the three most charmingly planned cities in the world. It was named after Queen Adelaide, wife of William IV.

Hay St 1897

81 (*above*) Perth, the capital of Western Australia, was named in honour of Perthshire-born Sir George Murray, Colonial Secretary when the site was chosen in 1829. Its development was held back until the mineral boom of recent years by the economic difficulties of its vast arid hinterland. When the city was incorporated in 1871 its population was only 5,000. Even when this photograph of its main commercial artery, Hay Street, was taken in the 1890s, the population was still only about 9,000. Judging by the Victorian frontages of the buildings at left, something of the construction boom of the 1880s hit Perth. It is noticeable however that the whole corner block is 'To Let by Tender' and its ground floor windows are boarded up. Perth would like to be a great centre, but still remains a pleasant colonial city with one of the best climates in the world.

82 (*opposite above*) Brisbane, the capital of Queensland, developed into a sprawling sub-tropical city after Moreton Bay penal settlement was closed down in 1839. It was named after Sir Thomas Brisbane, an Ayrshire-born governor of convict days. The city's long wharves on the wide Brisbane River made it suitable for shipment of enormous quantities of wool from the lush Darling Downs further inland. Favouring generally low buildings and wide shady verandahs, Brisbane did not participate much in the grotesqueries of boom architecture. In this photograph of Queen Street, taken in rather fierce sunlight in 1883, a formally dressed and felt-hatted resident poses near the gutter with his 'Salvo' tricycle. At extreme left is white-whiskered John McMaster, an early Scottish settler who was re-elected mayor nine times.

83 Retail shops in Australian cities have relied on imported goods for many years. Here is a typical colonial establishment, located in the Melbourne suburb of Fitzroy, of a man who imported all his cloth from Britain. Illustrations in his window show British fashions of the time (1866) which he copied as faithfully as possible. During the following decade it began to occur to Australians that perhaps they need not export all their raw materials and receive them back again in the form of manufactured goods. A minor 'Industrial Revolution' occurred, with the construction of many factories and imposition of protective tariffs to encourage people to use local cloths and other manufactures. But Australians still turn their eyes overseas on matters of fashion and taste.

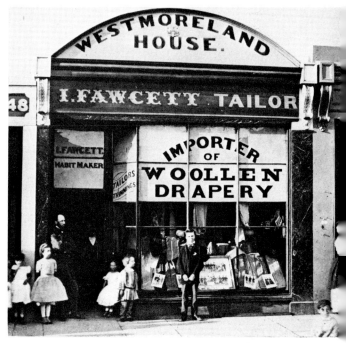

84 Surprisingly for a land of adventure and new frontiers, nineteenth-century Australia had just as much need as older countries for benevolent institutions of all kinds. Great stone buildings were erected in all leading towns and cities to accommodate the sick and 'deserving poor', many of whom arrived in that condition on fever-stricken immigrant ships. Here is the bright and cheery Children's Hospital in Adelaide, with its nurses lining the verandah and a one-legged boy playing with other inmates on the spacious lawns. The institution was separated from Adelaide Hospital in 1878 because, according to its chairman Sir Robert Barr Smith, 'they could not preserve the purity of the infant mind while a certain class of adult patients were admitted'.

EDUCATION

85 With all the emphasis given to pioneering activities, education of Australian children remained in a chaotic state until the 1870s. Church schools and private individuals catered for those who could afford the fees, but large sections of the population remained as illiterate as their British forebears. The two young ladies shown here at centre and right were the true pioneers of civilisation. They did their best to instruct youngsters at their little bush school, but at harvest or shearing time the pupils' services were usually required on the farm. This school seems in unusually good repair—unlike many it even has glazed windows. Only one child (seen with head hanging down) is without boots, an indication of a generally prosperous community.

86 Compulsory education became the law in most Australian colonies by 1880. Any children who did not attend church schools were compelled to undergo the 'free, secular and compulsory' tuition provided by the State. An enormous programme of school construction began: many of the buildings are still in use today. Here is the interior of the new public school at Hillgrove in northern NSW, in the district named 'New England' because of climatic similarities to the homeland. As with most buildings in the area, the school's walls and ceilings were lined entirely with beautiful cedar, which in those days grew profusely along the rivers but has now completely disappeared. The two school-mistresses standing stiffly at attention personify the era of rigid discipline in State schools which has only now begun to relax.

87 Australian pupils sometimes had difficulty in getting to and from school. When floods swept past the north-eastern Victorian town of Tallangatta in 1909, these children had to ease their horses gently across the floodwaters. The name 'Tallangatta' is aboriginal for 'many trees'. Some idea of the original forests can be gained from the surviving giant tree on the right, but the hillside behind has been almost completely stripped by settlers. In 1956 the houses at the foot of the hill were shifted and re-erected several miles away to make way for construction of new water storages.

88 With Australia's own little industrial revolution came the need for technical education of apprentices. Here the foundation stone is laid for the Gordon Institute of Technology at Geelong, Victoria, in 1891. For many years this included the only textile college in Australia. The man laying the stone is James Munro, a printer who emigrated from Edinburgh in 1858 and rose to become Premier of Victoria. Unfortunately he also started several building societies and private banks which crashed a few months after this photograph was taken. Munro hastily appointed himself colonial Agent-General, resigned as Premier, and fled to London.

89 Meanwhile church schools continued to educate children of the wealthy. Here are pupils of the Church of England Grammar School in Melbourne in 1876. When construction of the bluestone building began twenty years earlier, aborigines were still camping in the grounds under bough mia-mias. Among the school's original seventy-seven pupils was a boy who had been a powder monkey at the siege of Lucknow during the Indian Mutiny. Another pupil, aged twenty-two on enrolment, was a successful gold-digger paying for his own education.

90 Sydney established Australia's first university in 1851, with chairs in classics, mathematics and chemistry. Luckily the chemistry professor, John Smith, son of an Aberdeenshire blacksmith, was a keen amateur photographer. He took a notable series of photographs of the university's construction from 1854–60. The professor is seen here at extreme right timing the exposure. The main building, designed by a self-taught architect, Edmund Blacket of Southwark, Surrey, is generally acknowledged as one of the finest examples of Gothic architecture in Australia. At left, stone-carver John Popplewell chisels out a gargoyle, but the other two figures remain unidentified.

91 In Melbourne a prominent barrister, Irish-born Redmond Barry, provided in 1842 a free library service from his own house. Ten years later he persuaded the Victorian government to take over the function. As a result one of the world's great libraries of the time arose in Melbourne. Here we see part of the original reading room, which was greatly expanded from 1909–13 with a domed structure of similar size and shape to the British Museum. In 1860 the Melbourne institution began the world's first system of travelling box libraries for circulation among the popular mechanics' institutes and similar organisations.

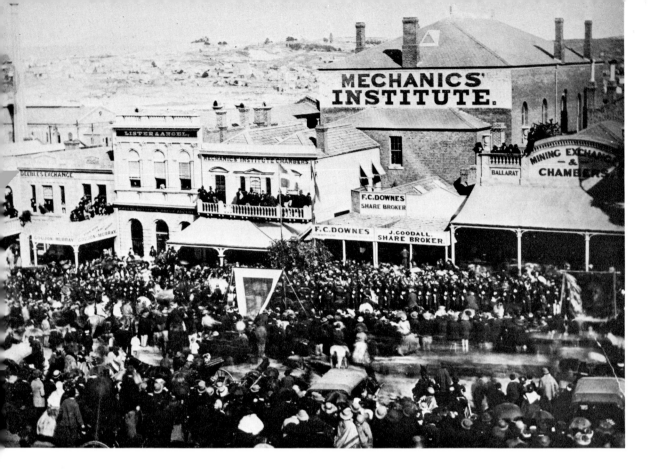

92 Australian mechanics' institutes were copied from similar movements for adult education in Glasgow and London. By 1840 practically every colonial capital had institutes giving low-cost lectures in science, history and the arts. By the 1860s the movement had spread to almost every country town with more than a few hundred population. Here we see the large crowd attracted to a function at Ballarat Mechanics' Institute in the 1860s, with crinolines greatly in evidence among female spectators. As State instruction spread, the institutes abandoned most of their educational activities and degenerated into mere recreation halls. A few years after its opening, the top floor of the institute shown here was turned into a billiard room, and the main hall was let for public entertainments.

LOYALTIES

93 From the earliest days Australia displayed an almost unquestioned loyalty to British imperial policies, matched only by the enthusiasm of New Zealanders. The great preponderance of British immigrants and descendants in both countries was no doubt the reason. Even small Australian towns made public displays of their devotion to Queen and Empire on every possible occasion. When Gawler in South Australia opened its new town hall in 1878, for instance, residents felt compelled to erect this arch praying that 'God Save the Queen'. The smaller arch on the right refers to the impending visit of Sir William Jervois, a British Army fortifications expert who was transferred to South Australia because he had embroiled Britain in the problems of Malaya whilst governor of the Straits Settlements.

94 To house the succession of British governors appointed to act in the monarch's name, each colony built government houses in the grand style with huge rooms for receptions, investitures, etc. The mansion shown here, built in Hobart from 1855–8, enjoys the distinction of having had its stone quarried and faced by some of the last convicts transported from England. This photograph was taken in 1867, when Queen Victoria's second son, Prince Alfred, Duke of Edinburgh, made the first royal tour of Australia. He was rapturously received everywhere but shot and wounded by an Irish immigrant in Sydney. The Duke is seen here holding the carriage reins. Behind him is the Tasmanian Governor, Sir Thomas Gore Browne, an old soldier who had precipitated the Maori wars when Governor of New Zealand, and been transferred to Tasmania as a result.

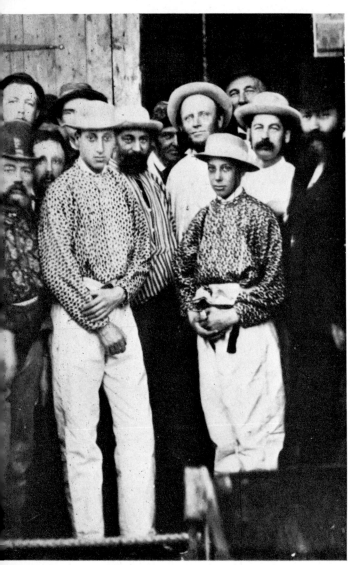

95 In 1881 Albert, Duke of Clarence, and George, Duke of York (later King George V) visited Australia as midshipmen. In NSW they shot kangaroos on a squatter's property. In Victoria they went down the Band of Hope & Albion Consols mine, from which £2,500,000 worth of gold had been extracted. Here the two princes are seen by the main shaft wearing miners' trousers and hats, and brightly coloured shirts. The bearded man in striped shirt is Vice-Admiral Clanwilliam, commander of the visiting naval squadron.

96 Australian nationalism began to assert itself in 1883 when Sir Thomas McIlwraith, an Ayrshire-born squatter who had become Premier of Queensland, decided to annex New Guinea. His aim was to forestall German expansion in the area. Lord Derby, Colonial Secretary of the time, disallowed the action. An almost unanimous storm of indignation swept the Australian colonies, forcing the British government to reverse its decision and take over part of the island in 1884. Here the British flag is hoisted at a missionary's house in Port Moresby by a Royal Naval detachment under Commander James Erskine. A tiny staff of six British officials was appointed. They were expected to administer the whole Protectorate, which was filled with savage cannibal tribes. Less than 100 years later, New Guinea was almost ready for independence.

97 (*above*) The third royal visit to Australia took place in 1901 for the opening of the first Federal parliament. The Duke of York was this time treated to quail shooting at 'Kilmany Park' in Gippsland, Victoria. He bagged 18 brace of quail during the morning, delighting Australians who admired good shooting. The Duke, on the right, rests on a fallen tree. Two other royal personages, King Billy and King Bobby of the almost-extinct Wurruk Wurruk tribe, came along to entertain him by throwing boomerangs and collecting as many 'tickpences' from the party as they could.

98 (*opposite above*) In Melbourne, temporary seat of Federal government, the Duke and his wife Princess May of Teck (later Queen Mary) were greeted by a succession of triumphal arches. With the Royal family's close German connections, Australia's 40,000 German immigrants were especially delighted. They raised this loyal archway in Swanston Street, Melbourne, fortunately ignorant of the fact that thirteen years later, on the outbreak of World War I, their newspapers and schools would be closed down, the Germanic names of their settlements changed, and many of them interned.

99 (right) After the Federation celebrations of 1901, Australians set about deciding on a site for a Federal capital. Because of interstate jealousies, the constitutional agreement between the colonies laid down that the site had to be more than 100 miles from Sydney. A royal commission was appointed to investigate competing claims. Its members are seen here (with assorted journalists) climbing a rabbit-proof fence to inspect a site near Albury, on the border between NSW and Victoria. After years of controversy, an old-established squatting station named 'Duntroon' was selected in 1909. Planning of Canberra, Australia's only artificially created city, began: its construction continues today.

SPORTS AND PASTIMES

100 The British who settled in Australia found fertile soil for most of their old-country recreations. Test cricket matches began in 1861 when a Melbourne catering firm organised the first English visit, and succeeded in making a handsome profit. In 1873–4 the great Dr W. G. Grace led the English team to Australia, combining the trip with his honeymoon. When he appeared on North Park Lands oval in Adelaide, as seen in this photograph, he was bowled after scoring one run. Torn between two loyalties, the British–Australian spectators didn't know whether to be disappointed or glad.

101   Picnics in the bush, on the beach or along quiet rivers were an always-favourite diversion in the generally sunny climate. This sylvan river scene in Sydney's Lane Cove (now a densely-settled suburb) was photographed about 1860 by Professor John Smith of Sydney University. Crinolines and top hats are much in evidence, but the man on the left wears a more casual felt hat with 'poultice' of muslin netting which could be lowered to protect the wearer against insect pests.

102   Croquet became popular in its present form at English country houses during the 1850s, and was exported to Australia within a few years. Here we see the first formal match which took place on a not very level paddock on New Year's Day, 1867. The ladies' cumbersome crinolines had now reached their peak and would soon disappear from fashion forever. This photograph was taken at Angas Town (today Angaston), a winemaking and mining centre in the Barossa Valley north of Adelaide, where Australia's first precious opals were discovered in 1849.

103   Most of its sports may have been de-
rivative, but in skiing Australia was a world
leader. When gold was found at Kiandra in
the Australian Alps in 1859, miners made
rough skis from local mountain ash and
used saplings as stocks. Here we see them
practising on what was then considered a
'high jump'. At 4,300 feet above sea level,
Kiandra became the highest permanent
settlement in NSW. Its Ski Club is one of
the oldest in the world. The only gold being
won there today comes from tourism.

104   Hunting was introduced into Australia
during the earliest days of white settlement.
Kangaroos, wild dogs and emus were used
as game in dangerous chases through the
untamed bush. Deer and foxes were acclimatised in the 1840s, and Sir Charles FitzRoy,
Governor of NSW from 1846–55, imported
pedigreed hounds from the Duke of Beau-
fort's kennels to improve the local breed.
Here is a hunt about to leave 'The Brocas'
at Woodville, South Australia, in 1870. The
efforts made to reproduce all the conven-
tions of the English hunt are obvious. Today, ironically, a large American-owned
automotive works covers much of the area.

105   With their generally warm climate and thousands of miles of sandy beaches, Australians quickly became addicted to sea bathing. In the early days nude swimming and sunbathing were common, but with the spread of Victorian 'respectability' the first laws were passed prohibiting nudity in public. In this photograph taken at the Sydney beach of Coogee about 1886, the bathers are wearing quite modern-looking swimming trunks. The bathing machines at the water's edge were imported from England so that ladies could change in privacy, to disport in the caged enclosure safe from sharks and presumably from male attentions. However, the group of young men seem to be waiting quite anxiously for the ladies to emerge and show their bare ankles.

106 Australians tried in vain for many years to stock their lakes and rivers with salmon. The first shipment of salmon eggs from England in 1874 hatched in the tropics and died. The next 50,000 eggs were hatched successfully in 1877 at this spot called the Salmon Ponds, on the Upper Derwent River in Tasmania. Released into rivers and lakes, the young salmon were devoured by natural enemies, and none survived. English trout however were acclimatised with great success and may still be caught today in some south-eastern rivers.

107 The wide rivers on which Australian capital cities were based also enabled Henley-type regattas to be staged each year. In Melbourne, Henley-on-Yarra began in 1904 and attracted up to half the city's population. In Adelaide, Henley-on-Torrens began in 1909 with twelve men's and four women's crews rowing. The local newspaper thought that 'No one could have recognised in that gay and beauteous picture the wilderness of tangled undergrowth and mudheaps' which had been replaced with the scene shown here.

THE UPPER CLASS

108 A common but mistaken notion about Australia is that after the gold rush it became an egalitarian society. Certainly Australians enjoyed more social mobility than people in the old world, but the new land still developed a considerable class of wealthy people with strong notions about exclusivity. In Sydney they built large mansions on nearby eastern hillsides and promontories such as Pott's Point, seen here in this 1890s view. The two- and three-storeyed mansions shown were the usual type of upper class architecture popular in both Sydney and Melbourne. Spacious lawns with statuary and peacocks led down to private boatsheds and the sparkling waters of Sydney Harbour. Today the area is covered with expensive mansions of a later era, but they are packed much more closely together.

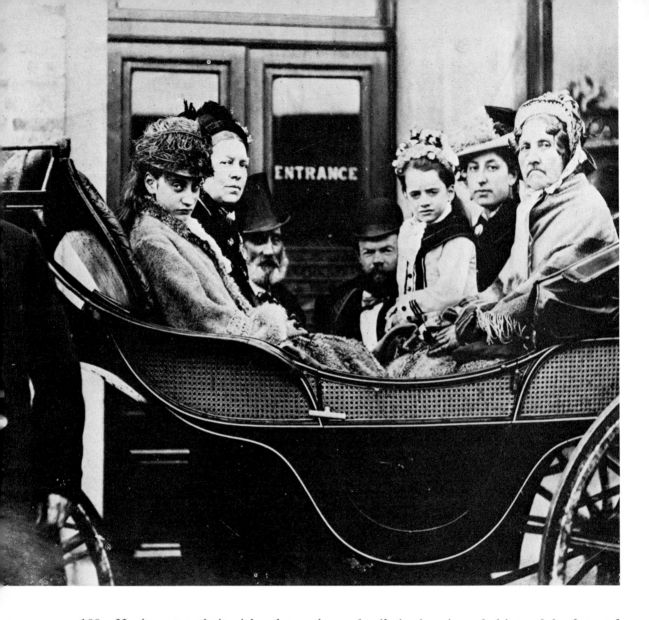

109   Having won their riches by various arduous methods, colonial *nouveaux riches* did not often wear them with any special grace. This wealthy family of the 1880s have progressed to their own carriage and footman (just visible at extreme left), are dressed fussily in the winter fashions of the day, and warmly covered with possum-skin rugs from the bush. But they do not look pleased at being photographed outside a Sydney hotel. Each face is a study in suspicion, world-weariness, or outrage.

110 In Victoria, wealthy squatters usually appointed managers to run their stations, and built town houses on the undulating hills near Melbourne, the capital. Here is one of the most charming of those mansions, 'Como', occupied by the wool-rich Armytage family from 1863. Charles Armytage is seen at left and his wife Caroline on the first floor balcony, while a footman waits by the front steps. This is one of the few squatters' town houses to survive the population explosion of the present era. The beautiful cast-iron lace and not-so-beautiful cement roof mouldings have gone. Today the house is the headquarters of the Victorian branch of the National Trust of Australia.

111 'Como' enjoyed a long span as one of the leading social centres of a socially-conscious city. This marvellous photograph, full of the vitality of the occasion, shows younger members of the Armytage family preparing to leave for a Melbourne Cup race meeting in the 1890s. All of the squatter's five sons and five daughters, plus a few friends, seem to be accounted for in this picture.

112 (*above*) Australia's most exclusive organisation, the Melbourne Club, was formed by squatters in 1838, two years after the capital's foundation. At first they took over small hotels to provide accommodation for members visiting town. Later they erected the present spacious but discreet building in the best part of the city's main commercial thoroughfare. This 1863 photograph—one of the rare interiors of the time—shows several of the colony's leading squatters sitting down to lunch in their top hats. An enormous saddle of beef awaits their attention on the centre table.

113 (*left*) As the wool aristocracy became entrenched, it was harder for newcomers to break in. Among those who tried and failed were two Canadian brothers, William and George Chaffey. In the 1880s they took up large areas of land along the Murray River, installed machinery to pump out millions of gallons of water daily, and sold irrigated fruit farms to thousands of new British settlers. Here the brothers are seen in the full flush of enthusiasm outside their new house 'Rio Vista' in Mildura. Technical difficulties and the crash of the 1890s killed the project, although the area itself later revived. Today the Chaffeys' old mansion is preserved as an historical museum.

114 (*above*) As colonies developed, politics provided a way into colonial 'aristocracy'.

Here are Sir Richard Davies Hanson and Lady Hanson at their home 'Woodhouse' early in the 1870s when Hanson was Chief Justice of South Australia. He was the son of a London fruit merchant, and had supported himself by journalism while qualifying as an attorney and solicitor in the 1820s. Emigrating to South Australia, Hanson was soon appointed to the Legislative Council, drafted the Act for responsible government in 1856, became Premier, passed the Empire's first law authorising marriage to a deceased wife's sister, then rapidly in turn became Chief Justice, Acting Governor, and Chancellor of the University. Meanwhile he wrote five books explaining the principles of Christianity. In the blossoming colonial milieu, such outstanding figures found full opportunity to utilise their talents.

95

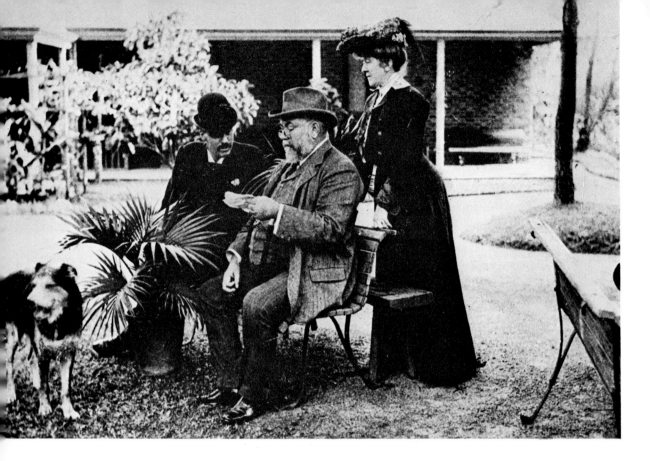

115 Similarly in Western Australia, a notable explorer named John Forrest rose to the top of society through the diversity of his talents. By 1874 he had explored much of WA's vast lands and been honoured by geographical societies throughout the world. Forrest was the natural choice as his colony's surveyor-general, became its first Premier under responsible government, and helped to bring his rather reluctant colony into the Federation movement of the 1890s. In Federal Parliament, Forrest lived to see a transcontinental railway (boasting the longest straight stretch of track in the world). In 1918 the explorer–politician became the first native-born Australian elevated to the peerage, taking the title of Baron Forrest of Bunbury. Here he is seen (centre) holidaying with Lady Margaret Forrest in WA at the turn of the century.

THE WORKING CLASS

116 Very few photographs seem to exist of the Australian working class in the nineteenth century. Perhaps photographers were too busy recording the images of great events and buildings to take much notice of the men who were carrying out the hard labour involved. Fortunately this Tasmanian picture has survived to show us what was meant by 'manual labour' in those days. Gigantic blocks of red granite for some mansion or city building are being painfully quarried with crowbar, chain, wedge and sledgehammer. Slate suitable for roofing was found in some areas, but most had to be imported from Britain as ballast in the holds of sailing ships.

117 Brick-making was one of the more valuable techniques imported into Australia by convicts from Britain. Although public buildings and gaols continued to be built of stone, brick houses were beginning to replace the early timber structures from the beginning of the nineteenth century. One of Australia's first trade unions, the Brickmakers' Friendly Society, was registered in Sydney as early as 1845. Here is an early brickworks outside the town of Bairnsdale, Victoria, with employees taking a break to smoke their clay pipes. The bands tied around some of the men's trouser legs just below the knee kept the ends from dragging in the clay. They were known as 'bowyangs', from provincial English 'bow-yanks' or leggings.

118 Here is another vivid reminder of the fearful amount of manual labour involved in nineteenth-century projects. This 1,000ft intake channel for the Bundaleer Waterworks in South Australia in 1897 had to be hewn out of the rocky soil with pick and shovel, and a 76ft embankment piled up with the aid of wheelbarrows. Construction techniques of this kind had barely altered since the days of slave labour in Egypt 4,000 years before. The result of this waterworks was to bring an extra 600,000 acres of land into production.

119 The first road link between South
Australia and Victoria was this Warren steel
truss bridge across the Murray River, com-
pleted in 1879 after fifteen years of disputation between the two colonies over cost and
site. As the long bridge neared completion,
workmen building it stopped to pose for
this photograph on the South Australian
side. Immigrants from many nations can be
seen, with a preponderance of Britons, Germans and Italians. A few youthful helpers
sit proudly on the first arch. Eight years
later the first train service between the two
colonies used this bridge.

120 'Benevolent asylums' were built in every large city to house workmen who failed to stand up to the long hours and heavy labour of ordinary jobs. But there was no benevolence for shirkers: each inmate was still forced to work to the limit of his ability, in order to earn his food. This photograph taken in the early 1860s shows inmates breaking up rocks for use as road metal at the Benevolent Asylum in North Melbourne. A journalist who spent several days there in 1876 found two Oxford men, several former surgeons and lawyers, and many former military officers among the broken-down workingmen. All had to sign wills handing over their assets to the institution.

SOCIAL CONFLICT

121 By the 1880s severe class tensions had developed in Australia. Working-class immigrants, especially the large proportion of Irish, adopted the outlaw Ned Kelly as a symbol of their struggle against 'oppression'. Ned was not much more than an intelligent horse-thief and bank-robber, but there is no doubt that he and his family were roughly treated by the police during his youth. Here is the famous bushranger, photographed in Melbourne Gaol on the day before he was hanged in 1880. The judge who sentenced him to death was another Irishman of a very different kind: Sir Redmond Barry, mentioned earlier as the man responsible for building the Melbourne Public Library. When Kelly was taken to the scaffold, he said calmly, 'I suppose it had to come to this'. The expression 'as game as Ned Kelly' became part of Australian folklore.

122   When the Kelly gang was besieged by police at Glenrowan, a small central Victorian town, another member named Joe Byrne was shot to death. His body was taken to the larger town of Seymour, and tied up against a door of the police station so that pressmen could take pictures. Here is the macabre scene, photographed by an onlooker who realised that the entire scene held more permanent significance than a mere picture of a bushranger's body. Note the children looking on. The smiling man at left wearing a 'hard hitter' was a press artist named Julian Ashton, later to become a prominent painter.

123 Bitter strikes rent the social fabric of Australia from the 1890s as trade unions struggled to improve wages and working conditions. One of the worst trouble-spots was the incredibly rich silver-lead mine at Broken Hill in outback NSW. When the owners attempted to reduce wages in 1908, union members picketed the mine and tried to dynamite communications with the out-side world. Here pickets march to the mine to the music of the town band. Their leader was the English socialist Tom Mann, seen here in the front row, third from the left, wearing a light-coloured suit and panama.

124 Unemployed men brought from the cities under police protection to work the mine were known as 'scabs', a term probably derived from an unpleasant disease which afflicted sheep. All good unionists loathed the scabs, whose efforts usually caused the strikes to collapse. When one died in the Broken Hill mine in 1909, union members erected this mock grave in the main street. 'Where he is we cannot tell/but may his soul rot in hell'.

125 In Australia a close alliance grew up between militant unionists and suffragettes. Here we see two union leaders: Harry Holland, who was gaoled for two years for his part in the Broken Hill strike, and A. Crawford, a prominent South African socialist. With them is Mrs Dora Montefiore, member of the London Jewish family which settled in Australia. The Woman's Suffrage League of Australia was formed at her home in Sydney in 1891. Largely through its efforts, women won the right to vote and sit in Parliament earlier than in Britain. However, no woman was actually elected to an Australian parliament until 1921, and very few since then. Australian men have always seemed to feel that women can have any rights they like as long as they don't actually use them.

126 Social conflict of a different kind occurred through the activities of temperance advocates. These earnest men were horrified by the hard-drinking habits of Australians, and tried to limit hotel hours or introduce prohibition. In the few areas in which they succeeded, the only result was widespread evasion of the licensing laws. In an attempt to provide alternatives, the 'teetotallers', or 'wowsers' as they became known, erected this marvellous pagoda at Melbourne's Flemington racecourse to serve soft drinks. The enterprise was a failure. By 1890 the pagoda was serving wine and spirits instead, and doing a roaring trade. Australians today remain among the world's heaviest drinkers, with a colossal road toll in which fifty per cent of drivers are drunk at the time of impact.

DEFENCE

127 With its meagre population scattered over three million square miles, Australia remained in constant fear of invasion by French or Russians in the nineteenth century or various Asian nations in the twentieth century. The costly British military presence began to diminish after convict days. To replace it, every centre of population raised its own volunteer defence force. Social pressures ensured that almost every active male 'joined up'. Here is the West Melbourne Detachment of Her Majesty's Customs Volunteer Rifles. It could almost be mistaken for an American Civil War photograph, and indeed was taken at about the same time, in 1861.

128 (*above*) Each colony also formed its own horse artillery groups, although the British government would not allow them to have any field guns until the last British regiment was withdrawn in 1870. After that date the movement spread rapidly, sometimes under the control of wealthy squatters who viewed the possession of artillery as the key to power in times of crisis (during the Queensland shearers' strikes of 1891–4 government artillery was actually deployed against them). Here is the Adelaide Artillery Battery in 1877, its members wearing blue Garibaldi jackets with scarlet facings, and proudly parading their muzzle-loading six-pounders. The stone building behind them became a repository which preserved government archives and some of the photographs used in this book.

129 (*left*) The British government insisted on retaining control of naval defences for several more decades. In 1869 and again in 1880, Royal Naval Flying Squadrons sailed around the world to relieve foreign stations. Visiting Sydney, they treated the colonists to a mock battle in the Harbour. Here thousands of residents gather to watch the display of British naval might which they were confident would keep invaders from their shores. The illusion lasted right up to 1942, when Japanese aircraft sank much of the British Pacific fleet, opening the way for bombing and submarine attacks.

130 (*above*) The Imperial idea of reciprocal military support received its first practical test in 1885, when news of General Gordon's death in Khartoum reached Australia. Most colonists reacted spontaneously, determined to teach the Soudanese that they could not massacre British invaders of their country with impunity. Strong forces of infantry and artillery were sent from the main Australian colonies. They arrived too late to see much action, but an interesting overseas tour was enjoyed by all. Here is part of the enormous crowd which jingoistically farewelled the NSW contingent in March 1885.

131 Being experienced bush riders, the Australians distinguished themselves in independent cavalry manoeuvres, developing a unique form of rough-riding operations. Some groups of mounted volunteers elected their own officers by a show of hands and deposed them if necessary by the same method. Traditionalists were horrified, but the practice paid off in the Boer War when Australian units were among the few who could meet Boer guerrillas on their own terms. Here a detachment of the Bushmen's Cavalry parades through Melbourne before leaving for South Africa in 1900.

132 After Federation, all political parties supported the introduction of universal military training for home defence on Swiss lines. Every young Australian male was given a rifle and uniform. Unless a conscientious objector (and magistrates approved few such applications), he was compelled to take part in weekly drilling and annual camps. Here we see the lads of Dulwich Hill Public School in NSW using their rifles for limbering exercises in a display during the early 1900s.

133 Lord Kitchener visited Australia in 1910 to advise on organisation of the Commonwealth's large forces. He observed that 'A great deal of training which would, in the ordinary course, have to be supplied to obtain an efficient soldier is already part of the daily life of many of your lads'. Looking to the possibility of action in the Middle East, Australians thereupon formed a Camel Corps to supplement the horse cavalry. Although men of the outback were used to handling camels, this beast at Menangle camp in NSW seems unwilling to co-operate in matters of Imperial policy.

134 When war finally came in 1914, Australians were fully prepared and even eager to volunteer for overseas service. Their finest symbol was the Light Horse trooper, mounted on his tireless bush horse, a little more disciplined than the old rough-riders, but still full of initiative and a crack shot from the saddle. So away they rode cheerfully to the great war which was to change the face of the modern world. Here in the foreground is Trooper W. H. R. Woods, one of the first men to be killed when the Anzac forces stormed the cliffs of Gallipoli. Australians, used as shock troops in many subsequent offensives, suffered 226,000 casualties during the war out of a total population of 800,000 men aged from twenty to forty—a higher proportion of casualties than any other country in the world, and every man of them a volunteer. The brutal result was quickly transmuted into a tradition of glory, but in truth the flower of Australia's manhood had perished. A long sickness of cynicism and despair, a numbing feeling of futility, overcame the nation. It has only begun to lift in recent years.

INDEX